The Bad Wife Handbook

WESLEYAN POETRY

The Bad Wife Handbook

Rachel Zucker

Wesleyan University Press

MIDDLETOWN, CONNECTICUT

Published by Wesleyan University Press, Middletown, CT 06459

www.wesleyan.edu/wespress

Printed in the United States of America

5 4 3 2 1

Library of Congress Cataloging-in-Publication Data
Zucker, Rachel.
The bad wife handbook / Rachel Zucker.
    p.   cm. -- (Wesleyan poetry)
ISBN-13: 978-0-8195-6846-5 (alk. paper)
ISBN-10: 0-8195-6846-5 (alk. paper)
I. Title.
PS3626.U26B33 2007
811'.6--dc22   2007019778

In spite of
& because,
Joshua Goren

Contents

. . . synonyms do not exist.

—*Donald Hall*

Monogamist

A human being can't compare
size and brightness

on two occasions. So we say
the moon has a dark side.

We say *the tide twice a day.*
I say *that man there, so unlike*

my husband.

The Museum of Accidents

The school girl's tights speckle
in the rain. In the city

the sparrow on sparrow feet skips
across my path, legs invisible.

We are bound. Similar,
       indistinct forms called bodies,
       our Milky Way's spiral arms—
       stars, nebulae, matter—

              bound
to great disaster.

Codary

Once he was a type, kind, tide,
but became a singularity.

I stopped breathing.

Where the husband's orbit overlaps: darkness.
No light can be shed on what lies beyond this

gravitational sheer,
harsh polarity

of wanting.

The Secret Room

Isn't hidden. Nor filled with goods
or bodies. This feeling—

⌈strip the wallpaper,
knock for panels⌉

I can't explain it—is always,
I think his gaze made it. I say

what I don't intend
so as to say something of

this tending, tendency, tender
unsayable place I mean to take him.

Firmament

Below his clean shadow:
a sunlit prairie. A wheat field

from the air: plush and temperate.

The breeze is a brave caress. There is
something I see in him: tip, edge, hint

—the skin of it. Shifting wheat

over soil over cavern over water
over igneous over molten.

Monogamist

Riding a bike down a flight
of steps misnames them,

reveals their lusty gravity.

Have you heard that Brontosaurus
is a Camarasaurus head on

an Apatosaurus body?—my
love's like that: shaped,

named beast did, did not exist.

They should be called falls, this
plummet.

Galaxies Rushing Away

I'm trying not to try to
get him into bed. Instead I try

but the husband flinches when I
and flinches when I say

I love you and I do
love you but say

I'm meeting a woman named Kate.
Then, off to the winebar, order

sancerre, nice summery white at $7/glass;
he, me, and vast millions are fast,

—red shift getting redder, every galaxy
from every galaxy, vow, promise, primordial

atom—rushing faster, all on our way
to greater disorder.

Axon, Dendrite, Rain

When he speaks I am allowed to look at him.
Let this perfect conjure slide over (all over)
the thought reaching out to my loud now—
                                    I want to—
but find no way to make my hands
natural, accidental. I try to make his skin
a chaste idea. But even his gloves, made from slaughtered
goats, their pliable kid leather become a bias-cut
slip, myelin sheath, the impulse *jumps*
node-to-node, too fast for capture.
                                    The body.

Less, less real. I am aware of wanting
to look at him. In the long space
in which others speak I cannot look at him.

                take your clothes off

And I do. In dream after dream, except
last night when I'm running a long way
in the rain and, basketball in one hand, he
stands watching. And when he watches—
I run and run, do not wake up
but that—(there,) that, that, that: rain
at my window, husband in my bed.

Rhyme, Lascivious Matchmaker

Each time I try to—
here comes my husband again and

my mind, I'm describing; context.

Forgive me, anemone, my green clearing.
He is no still pool, but actual.

If I showed him my skull below the skin
then threw out the skin, would he wipe clean

the bone? A thin gold wire
prevents my jaw from metaphor or . . .

His v-neck suggests—
The bruised way he sits—

What to do with his lips—

Hermeneutic

The sea is supposed to be something
more than a saline menagerie.

I thought to be full of feeling
rather than *with child* was

mutable, could stay small, but now I'm
desolate, fleeting, pierced with this blunt

fissure. My babies left a narrow passage
where longing festers. And here he entered.

Brutal shunt, my heart fills
with sea water. Involuntary muscles

seize, shudder, refuse to scar.

The Tell

The basketball makes him not my husband
and saying so in poems makes me

the bad wife. Where is the private, i.e., impassive
mask I purchased for my wedding

but then forgot to wear?

My mind wrote me a letter requesting to be
left out of it. My body sent flowers

and a note: "sorry for your loss."
But both paid to see the flop and stayed in 'til the river.

Better to fold the winning hand than fall in love
with your cards, says the husband.

Where I Went Instead of Paris

In the city, out windows, I fit his face
onto the faces of other men and boys

and look away before it fades.
I have learned to fly by running fast,

though the waking body won't comply.
His face is the face of all men

not my husband; I see him everywhere.

In the next dream I shave my head
and find my skull misshapen. In the next dream

I am raped in the elevator. The doorman
steps over my body. He has your face.

Wife, Wife, Duck

I'm not sure what this could be called "doubt"
but that's too simple these clouds: grayer than white

(the white sky behind) like the sky at evening.
To wish the best for someone

I love might mean leaving
or leaving him alone. To wish for

him. Wish for him to—

It looks like rain means
it's not raining.

It Took 24 Hours to Make the Moon

I forgot to think of him today.

Made of carbon, oxygen, calcium: you, him, I, stars.

When a Mars-like body and Earth collided
within hours was a protoplanet named Moon

and a planet moved away.
For days

I forget.

Mantle, core, ocean, air, I
am made of our

—air, air, air and air—
carved-out crater of impact.

Alluvial

They say God's voice in the city
sounds like a man but in the desert

sounds like a woman. His voice, the spine
of nighttime, sounds like water.

Rock grazed by streamlets long enough
will sunder. One word against my sternum and

I unzip.

Monogamist

I've fallen _____ with him, stupid
cliché, with his dark blue

officewear. Maybe

I just love my little boy too much—he
looks like him—itself a grievous treason.

Just ask my older son. Ask
the husband. Ask anyone. Ask

the language for one decent synonym
and watch it stutter: perseveration,

obsession, attention to detail
aren't love exactly nor is

chastity enough punishment.

My Beautiful Wickedness

Someone dropped a house on me
and stole my blood shoes.

The girl with her skipping and singing
comes to kill me. What then will become

of my spells, sole treasure I possess?

What I see when what I see
is not there—I know he feels it.

Looking at him like this

isn't a spell to make him
love anyone

but might. All the good wife
wants is to go home.

When no one watches
I teach the dog to fly.

Floating Wick in Petrol

I am too happy to see him.

Someone must be blamed. Perhaps
the therapist or my marrying young.

Say, are you really this beautiful?

I dream a woman puts a gun in my mouth
to make me choose—lustrous, sleek, sexed.

Next a jade green sandal from a bottom
drawer. Suede wedge with straps

that wind around my shin. My foot
in the smooth cradle is lavish, ignitable.

Please, say you are a dress I can put on for tonight,
say you are a gun or untouched leather

purse, a beaded belt or denim
patch or felt-bottomed box or basted hem, say

you are a spiral binding or photo of a forest
framed in beeswax, say a hat pin, say a buckle

say a gun or polished knob, say anything

Bridle

I promised to stay steady,
but who knew the rage

of arbors?

Forests, groves, flagpoles,
Stand, we told them. *Stay.*

When we set up the blocking,
marked my toe-stops with tape,

I can't describe it—
how my shoes abrade,

fit, like casket.

Thought, Antithoughts

I've nothing to hold him,
suspect I've been dreaming—

a woman awake, her
husband breathing—she wants

to be anywhere.

He's a man
who happened to notice

I made him want
to play guitar

but he didn't. This is the winter
the husband started snoring

and science said free will
is a feeling we believe in.

Post hoc confabulation.

I must get up and attend
the microorganisms.

Sex

Wane, wax, wobble.
My mind is a map of hunger.

They say Abulafia could stop his heart
with one letter. *Alef*

lodged in his semi-lunar valve.

Small *e* after breath
is what I do to keep living.

What Is Not Science Is Art Is Nature

I am dreaming a hole right into the voice of God.
Straight into the dark place where my children were made

but can't follow me back to. Right into the room
whose windows are too high up to see out,

though the sloped roof is too low for me to stand up.

In New York snow is unusual, arrives like childhood
memories that might not have happened, disappears

without changing anything. But do we say,
when it snows, because some countries

don't believe in snow, *I dreamed
of snow?* No, we say the news was right or wrong.

We say this strong desire for a window—huge square
glass through which a child standing up in a crib

at night alone in a room at the bottom of a flight
of stairs far from the mother in winter sees:

a Greenwich Village garden cast in urban glow,

quiet, because snow in the '70s was enough
to make the city slow and mute—is real.

So, say it really happened. That doesn't mean

it will again or did. Or that the dream
doesn't make you ordinary.

Freud Had Sex but Jung Had God

I take water
into my lungs

in lieu of him, want for air,
have none and not

because a good wife rose up in me
or a sharp right turn, bright

discipline befell me: I wanted
sugar and salt in equal measure

one making the other desperate
the now tasteless by turns desperate

this was this wanting of course
it was the kind of snow that never

sticks—O blizzard! wild sky at wit's end—

but when I look again
the street is barely stained

(sugar, flurry, salt, drift)

and the flat, clean air swears
snow never fell here.

Squirrel in a Palm Tree

}

up, out of the sentry box over the parapet, bastion, rampart, breastwork

⌈don't think "I have left them . . ."⌉

draw and look, lift—erase, draw and lift and lift and lift

an erasable slate
the velum top sheet takes away

⌈"left them"⌉

}

up, over the country

      the edge of coast and further out the clouds like stones in deep waters
      a river delving the lush green
      marsh an amorphous rum babba, soaked and spongy
      grasses and cattails misstate the surface

      the cabin has the sharp inhale of opening a gift

Ø

high ceiling (blue) and pink and gray striped walls shape me

    make a naked Alice in the bath

        big and tiny
        here and far away

        a wonder the body fits
        so mythic is the mother-absentia

        tundra of abandon

I suffer the gift,   silence,

                for once, nothing happening

    none using my name to mean anything

∅

bed as wide as it is long

the night inhuman calm

the outlets and picture frames and decorative plates are safe

the bathtub and mirror and doors and linens

I am as light as negligee

have not my army's entourage

∅

on Sunday I will step back into the living room littered with toys
the two boys happy/shy/mad to see me
but like I dawdled in the shower

like I never was anywhere but ready to answer
where is my?
can't find the . . .

look here, the light through the sycamores and dense magnolias
live oaks tasked with spanish moss

a veranda you reach through a twelve-foot window

be real

∅

unnaturally light
like a various gravity exhibit at a science museum
my mother has a necklace made of severed reeds
that seem to weigh
less than air

they look like bird teeth or shell splinters

                    —Haiti? Australia? Peru?

she can't remember where she got it

but the stones—emerald rough from Sri Lanka
on the bookshelf near the kitchen; square, flat rock from Arizona
on the mantle in the bedroom—those she knows by heart

a life of picking things up and bringing them elsewhere

Ø

here is the tree of my thirtieth birthday:
a palm between two sycamores

      the pineapple-totem trunk is a woven present
      fronds rustling to offset loneliness
      squirrel feasts on hope

∅

alone, the room gets smaller despite there being fewer people
the TV approaches like a hopeful lover

                     let us, I say to myself, consider the children objectively, which is
           impossible:

the boys who are babies create a slavish planet. this means I am bending and lifting and every each moment listening
for disaster which is silence where his "dadaka" and "teka-te*kah*" pause is surely climbing or choking or considering
mischief

      on guard, keeper! be lively!

anything which requires concentration is danger—

so drag myself to watchfulness with a stab of catastrophic thinking so tired, delighted
I've half a mind to leave them and no mind left to do it and nothing to spare of this utter love

mother in a foreign   make this   real

Ø

some day they will leave *you*

and you will visit the kingdom of adult concerns and never leave
and will want to and will dream of night wakings and tiny spoons of temperate cereal on hands and knees for spilled
cumin seeds you will remember the every night of tiny things back in boxes and on shelves and under and in and the
ache ache ache of your back as he learns to walk or the relief of finally squatting in a parking lot to nurse him stop
that wail

a woman with young children is not a woman but a mammal, salve, croon, water carrier

she has a prize they all desire

lift, lift, life

Ø

if there are nests discarded on the sidewalk
I step around them knowing what it costs to weave one

once my shadow was the shape of a bear or egg with arms and legs
now slim and bony the boys sucked the melon-sweet milk right out of

        a letting, flesh mongers

and if the nest, a relic, outlasts the wind, rain, marauders,
it is always the cupped halo of ambivalence

desire won over by desire is not the same as satisfaction nor lust nor yet resolve
I don't believe in happiness

∅

I am equally and at once estranged from the person I knew as I
and from the mossy being made so carefully

the child becomes a wedge between actions and self like a cyclone of gauze wraps himself around my mothering
and makes a hollow form

                                    shape: human

cocoon around a maelstrom

∅

in New York the apartment's windows face south and my son knows little of the sunset
only that at night it's on the other side of the world

sleep with me, he says
I like the other sheets, he says
lime in my sippy cup?
anything to keep me

object of desires, I never satisfy because my body is impractical,
boundaried, impermanent

here, on the balcony, dusk draws the bundled leaves on winter trees
like hanging planters or Christmas ornaments

twenty minutes later the leaves are hedgehogs,
the branches: flaws and fractures in the skin of twilight

now on the other side of the world, the sun's fiery descent means little when witnessed
less when missed

        perception or staying is a mighty effort

Ø

if the language would slip I could see what limber chance remains me
                              but is always my chaperone

the moon is so full it must recline
the hip is the location the child claims
                    and aches

from use, from absence, the whole pelvis an isosceles arrowhead
barely a ledge the arm comes to scaffold him, the elbow buffer from gaudy onlookers
the breast becomes the shy boy's brow-rest—does he remember the Cyclops wonders?

I remember his greedy squeezing kneading tiny nail edge
my love a tinderbox   inflamed, viral

            obese,   inhale

                                                                        I miss . . .

when the child falls forward and catches himself with his hands, stands carefully, bunches his face: *fine, fine,* I get to
hold him now and kiss his palms and put my nose against his cheek

∅

when away from my tree I want to brag the treasure

smooth green globe
before the husk mars innocence

monumental nut
where can I bury such bounty?

the sugar-milk is too much at once and must be dealt with
but there is no dividing beauty, no rationing

I must escape my reputation for hoarding—so in love with the heft of the Asian pear,
the lusty hue of the persimmon, I keep and keep until they spoil
                                        —*Crack it!*
these edibles, not memories,
the fontanel bones of his skull about to close

Ø

some women cherish the fathomless want of infants

as it is all around me I cannot muster judgment and having been stayed from my sentence these three days by a stutter
of double dashes -- I --

  am still,   I

on either side of the long spine lie two shallow ditches walk your finger tips along these furrows but never pressure
the raised column holy like the horizon it is the going and the getting and the lifting and the carrying the bending
and listening kneeling and squatting it is my fingers' careful sweeping the alphabet floor mat at four am for the rub-
ber binky it is the way my body in his twin bed tricks him to sleep the way I tucked his baby face against my belly and
stood and stooped and swung like a mechanical gadget and set him down and made the back stay hunched so the hand
could stroke his hair and sleep him and stayed when the back protested and when the mind tried to make sense the
body stopped it

      my love is the bent body, the mastered spine

{

the coast is a sure painter's mark
but the horizon   is nothing human

from this height the flat expanse of farms and plots and houses, speckled towns
like the oyster, lime, and sand sidewalk they call "tabby"

then like flecks of polished shell the tilted glance makes the settled patches rise
like lily pads on tree-green ponds, the roads lascivious zippers

and the sun through the horizon crawl-space may be the moon
for it is everywhere a glowing ring and cannot be a star rather some bulb
just this width greater than the earth's diameter

whether my body is in conflict with the plane's intention is irrelevant

                    my children at this remove are figures, figments

the difference between here and there

{

planes always wanted to

lighthouse, cliffside, pride

they carry but do not mother

{

20 miles from LaGuardia the houses are little studs punched into denim, no longer in fashion

the tugs make snags in the nylon surface of the ocean, the houses and trucks
along the capillaries, when,

     oh my—

          the fortress edges of Battery Park, airshaft depressions of empty lots
          and unbought air rights and

               the Empire State building   amazing
          with her glinting, ramrod posture, suddenly

alone above her waist-high charges

Annunciation

traveling or intussusception (an introduction)

there is an inside as in my child as I see him or, earlier, felt him—
myself a stricture outside the real— there is an outside as in his real face, fake
laugh, mimic cry and, before, the body bigger: what it looked like—

there is an inside: my mind at night a plan the word escape, and outside:
I in bed the body in place, in my place I put myself, the body, in, a stand-in, harbor—

there is inside a bric-a-brac system: faith or habit, what turns my head,
fires along the ocular chiasm— pinpoint this/that while the hand goes thoughtless
after: grab and pull, peel and core, locate and obtain—

balcony (florence)

the fact (Italy) being around us— we go-betweens— the sky an impossible duomo
or drop cloth over the cage— traverse and return— we traverse and rest— one thought
at the edges transgresses— what is disillusionment?— a young man whistles by
on a bike— Catholics believe in impure thoughts— even saying is happen— but I want
to believe in interiors: spaces others don't conceive—

the bicycle is overtaken by a moped and that by car and that by bus and everywhere
the crowd teeming, seeming from here human, a given, a context, granted—
each particular (woman with two small dogs stops, searches for key in purse) is a point
on a tangent (man on moped) of some veiny larger— you are out, I am here—
within the city wall— *portes*— breaks in the wall, notional membrane on the map—

santa maria del carmine

you become is— and suddenly are— [we] not just an emblem, my other—
you tried to avoid saying always avoiding I tell you to say, say *it* but I also avoid
because emblem and becoming symbol but suddenly between Masolino
and Masaccio, symbol and symbol, you suddenly become and are— at home the baby
avoids sleep, crying, wanting to say but not knowing how, let's avoid him
for the while occupied, crying his own space— meanwhile my intestines and internal
have returned to normal although the package somewhat slack my mind sets
to tighten and look around, look for— then at night, last night, you suddenly are
and not this time the obstacle but rather good company, a voice in the room—
ribs heavy on the bed my body a cage pushing both ways voice in my head open mouth slips
out— suddenly is— *is*— and edged, mountainous—

bed

cannot call it forgiving this thin pad over wood but when you knock on the cage
of my body I do not break no less forgiving I do not crush or falter this is what it is to be
knocked-up? though mostly the motion is down and I am 'under' and then
don't think just am until that woman breathing isn't me, baby at the foot of the bed not mine
body not around or inside but me and rather than situation I feel you are a problem
force to reckon with I am you are breath, then an occasional motor bike, long gasping night
then nothing my body inside-out and in the after notice the quiet as it closes in

avoid

in the morning gone again and only body, presence but not is— is this
what I married? you: here, a given— *is*, as in: situation, situated (choice made before)—

some search for the soul or mind in the body: I think it is a membrane around
the void, scrim between skin and bones— I feel it lingering, clinging— not deep but
rooted to itself— not leaking (contained) not touching— one cannot touch it—
doctors open but do not find, open but not reveal—

situation: we are two within a larger— each around an empty inside a pulled skin—
sometimes in contact we have no choice but choose proximity to make a smaller
system— parcel, context— block out the bright or heavy rain verdant— what I am trying
to describe is disappearance: what happened and how you can be and invisible,
be but not is— even the language knows it, fact without gerund— voice with edges
but not edgy—

balcony

there are two sides two centers therefore an interior or, instead, between—
a space that is neither, a passage, a pause— of moment is the thing exposed but not within—
here we walk as if together as if— scent of testosterone, then gone— another's
Madeleine, another epic— I am outside and in and up and on— who knows perhaps I am also
in your thoughts as you, your stand-in, are in mine?

later the terrace is chilly, exposed and the bells make the air softer the light pinkish— there is
an advantage to self-possession but I can't remember what— the clouds watercolor
ambivalent, a misplaced seasky far from the sea— not at home but having brought it
with us— who snuck it into the luggage, what pocket? under whose saddle?—
the silver cup of longing displaces me— I, almost unseated, wanted to make not an emblem but
what, what is there that is real?— if you are a situation it is what you are— I tell
the story and we are still here despite being *dépaysés* or out of country, dizzy as if trying to find
my way with only a mirror and not eyes—

santo spirito

the angel humbles before her and she with her book raises her other hand
as if to a man offering stolen watches, "not interested"— she looks comfortable,
      perhaps the chair was made specially— between them the showy tiles, a vase
with three dark flowers, her hand stays as it is—

when the child is born she becomes younger, more innocent, naïve, she wears
her blue cloak constantly— becomes younger until, in the end, the *pietà*, who knows
      but she *is* younger than the son—

what if you only had one scene to work with, say the nativity or the annunciation
and it had to say everything and was the only story you had— the angel over and over,
    slightly different tiles, flat or this time perspective— it has will have the same ending
but the curve of her hand, no thank you, slope of her gaze say something new— today
    she hides behind the scene— the angel's arms crossed at the wrists like a double bow
but also, look again, like an embrace—

how dare he with his golden curls the angel presumptuous his down-turned eyes and
folded wings— he has already removed his shoes and has beautiful feet— she alone, not yet
    of child, in some grand palazzo says shyly, no thank you, one hand poised in half prayer,
(open, possible) not altogether proper— the other stubborn on the book— not yet a virgin
    her blue is French almost gray—

then, when time flattens, the big fish comes to swallow Noah, ark and all, and Mary
in her blue kimono goes to Holofernes— someone has taken her desire and used it to fashion
    a child— deep, deep into the colonnade one vertebrae at a time someone has taken her
and left a little changeling in exchange, now a virgin except that in the flimsy of her negligee
    a knife and map of the jugular

portrait of unknown

a pomegranate, calla lily, sprig of rosemary, meanwhile we do not say but rather tell
and tell around the jelly-centered heart— come away! soft sugary evidence— what is the form
of woman besides body?— there were flowers a given and a garden— one must
pay to enter but may leave as one desires— unencumbered by regret or so they said but the story
refuses to unfold peacefully— the past a torn ticket or smeared receipt— the story refuses
to reveal or adhere but is dropped behind, a savory trail, birds circle wearily— I should have
brought pearls or marbles or pen caps— instead or *in her place an anemone*— where I
go down springs up a delicate poison to mark descent: flower between my lips—

cloister or "vietato toccare le rose"

the church no matter how big is the idea of space but not space— they have painted
the windows which are sharp and pedantic, they have hung paintings in all the alcoves
and in the paintings are windows and in the windows people look out at pictures
of the world— they are therefore never going out and when pictured the child pale
white and shrunken, the mother young and small in her dark blue, there is no escaping
the painting the world not real as it is allegory this place a huge tomb— turns out there is a price
for leaving— now we have found other places small places banal to inhabit
and it is not so easy to break a gash in the wall and look out—

outside, the cloister is: breath, sinus, the habitable— here day comes into its own
and takes me with it— into itself, a light blue with folds and tiny flaws— who knows
if the column reaches up or down or even reaches as much as is and is again
but this time not a cage— the roof surrounds what is not roof, the walls create an inside-out:
cloister— a woman could breathe here, someone celibate— building outside,
air in— a woman could live among other women exposed and enveloped— but this is
never what I choose— a boy drawing, long sleeved thermal under a short sleeved T,
like a fallen Mormon looks up as though to sketch what is not there— don't touch the roses,
don't trample the grass— it's *interdit, vietato*— and the past meanwhile that shabby habit
insinuates and even the light blue day cannot protect me—

ministries of grace (kansas city)

        the wings are not attached— background— he wears a scarf, almost a bib or like
a young boy planning to rob a train in his backyard, bandana— the sperm of God
        in straight gold rays streams in through the window— later Christ, a naked homely
child, unlike anything in the natural world—

        Gabriel always enters from the left or from inside the painting the right— which one
or where are you?— I wasn't waiting just reading on my own writing letters— I wasn't waiting
        for the natural world to perform or people to take their places I wasn't waiting
was occupied otherwise when came this new work some holy imposition—

        hotel room when I finally sleep I have that dream there is a room in my apartment
I've never seen it is my favorite dream this time the room is tiled: floor, walls and ceiling—
        square white tiles the walls at odd angles like corners of an old house— the dream says
I will spend a year in there making light stick to film and paper in low or no light then out
        through the light-safe door to look at what I made, will hit my head and feel lucky—

annunciation (new york)

        when the situation became upside down everything changed: perspective,
counting, there was none of it— I cannot even say unprepared the mother father angry
        not wanting and not able to say solution or consequences when all I meant to say is,
"this happened"— one could gloss perhaps a history but truth is who knows— who was
        that masked man his wings folded back in the night no candle to read by
the baby sleeping, quiet—

when I woke up it occurred to me then at night and at morning and afternoon the calendar
        staring its hard boxes— go in pull up the blanket around the baby he is too sweet
sleeping the blanket will not kill him despite the doctor— I must sleep also but afraid, this way
        fear this way fear leads two ways is not reliable— how did this? who did we?—
I must think, sharpen my mind even on a stray arrowhead it is worth remembering— I saw
        the angel it is a sick joke I was not I said interested in this or in that fucking angel—

        but no one will believe me—

Mary was reading (an anachronism) probably religious texts (improbable) when
Gabriel interrupts— humbled? he thinks himself his message more important must insist—
who is this woman of leisure in grand palazzo— what father taught her letters what
sire built the chair, suitor gave her leather bound volumes— I write faster until progesterone
pulls me under not time left— haze of motherhood— she's never seen again reading
or in repose, only holding: He alive, He dead, she holding, watching, surrounded— there is no
grace in this but work though I can't say I put up much resistance— mine a small
palazzo: marriage, port-a-crib at the foot of the bed blocking the exit— one hand feeble
before me, window already open, gold rays inside— I was am tired— there is nothing
to say, it is not about language— so get up, get up now what we do the only matter—

central park

        Jesus in the water does not look clean or fish-like or marine at all but only unafraid
as if he knew he had gills as if the oxygen in the sea were the same as air— I will not
      get clean but will drown I have one name only— a spider rests in his lazy cross of web
high up above the park bench— one branch to another— why in the world did the dove's
      tiny sprig comfort Noah, he had no gills—

                      I was not the subject but location—

      and these first buds, some plot within my very death, I hardly mind
have eyes to see: this ravishing, there may not be another like it—

sighting (nova scotia)

        you say it is a cloud formation not land but when two mornings later true mist
rolls in we know we are missing something— was it just a strip of darker water over
        the horizon— a craggy one line list of the missing: sex, romance, tourism, humidity
obscured by the new baby, the baby, discipline, weather, will— our work, our work,
        the distance to town, the meager produce, slippery rocks and what was for a moment
a whale on second look just driftwood behind a buoy—

        the sea today has got a grudge against something— look! I say, waves! and the baby
waves— a gull on the low-tide rocks tries to lift but is blown back and forced to land—
        again and again— wanting, wanting in spite of—

it was not where bodies washed up, were fished out or brought ashore but where
we landed, marine and rocky— the sea calm, a bay, but the tides in and out with fierce
ambition— two gray chairs in the sun almost touching— dry rocks, mossy rocks,
seaweed covered and glossy close to the edge—

inside, the celibacy of pages turning, a computer-hum in the short utopia of a sleeping child—
the I-mama growing and looking longingly out of doors through the big wall windows—

the town has no church, library or playground just pale lettuce or fiddleheads for a short
season— the top rocks shiver their tidal pools, a striped-back bird like a skunk—
and on thick mist days I think of Cordelia, imprisoned, wishing— and not for Lear and not
for Burgundy and not the King of France but no one bothers asking—

once a virgin, one can change and change back— but once a mother
always— she was not a conduit or vessel but holy messenger, chosen— they were all
taking and wanting and swore his leaving made him stay, would make him
deep in the heart of the people— but what mother wants a child deep in the heart
of the people— how then should she guard him, watch, gather?

his body a seed within her, a tadpole or parasite— docile, lazy child: animal born
in captivity— what was new about him? only that he made her a mother,
round with waiting— patient like all famous women, her blue like the part of the sea
none survive— when she looks again he is a trilliant-shaped glimmer, bitter
jewel— what is real? house, body, tide?— the water is too cold for anything, the house
velvety, badly decorated— it is a sin to stay inside— be rather by the edge—
shorelined—

in cities elevators never fail to sicken— too many things inside others—
but here, the sea itself and its ambivalent rushing— back and forth, towards
and fast away does not unsettle— largely a house myself, I have, when seated,
a kind of balance and from my gray chair are everywhere windows and color
and in the distance the thin blue promise of what I know must be another coast—

Children- (if it Please God)—Constant companion, (& friend in old age) who will feel interested in one,—object to be beloved and played with.—better than a dog anyhow.—Home, & someone to take care of house-charms of music and female chit-chat.—These things good for one's health.—but terrible loss of time.—

Marry, Marry, Marry Q.E.D.

—*Charles Darwin*

The Rise and Fall of the Central Dogma

I. REPLICATION

> Is the Soul just a notion, a drug?
> —*Alice Notley*

That it was politically impossible.
That there was an alternative.
That I would stay.
That the lighthouse was useful.
That I would leave.
That germs infiltrate.
That babies before conception.
That the white collar means concern; the long beard, the shaved head, intensely dyed garment.
That sex is an effective way of generating warmth.
That a bay mare and wild iris are unalike.
That the gaze is not chemical or electricity requires a conductor.
That a saucepan and spoon are better toys.
That the office is not a tundra and not a mirage and not.
That traits are inherited.
That ideas will save us.

That a mother's face is not her mindset—
even the infant knows it. And yet we put her
on television, donate particle scopes.

I tell you there is a secret world.

That children too young to walk must be carried.
That weight can be assessed or described.
That speech is directional.
That God knows genomes.
That the phone in and of itself is not a husband.
That a dream is not reason to evacuate.
That the man's death was made of 53 wing bones and the well-planned curve of highway.
That walking one way was, or this way is, or that the curved back of old bones as seen through
    a low slit of window is anything but interference: the spiking lights on the mute-stereo or turned-down
    cardiogram.

The city is less "planned" than *exposed*
    and emerges, one bodega, tenement, row house,
park, highway, until they've pushed out ambiguity.

I believed greatly in the grabby valence of molecules,
tricky protons and funny quarks, my son's invisible puppies:
Muffin, Apple, Muffin, and Lemon.

The map's coincidence; the body's freak resemblance.

The *They never told me* of women in labor or
Here we are under the chuppah.

A flat bed excavator builds its own scaffold.

Secret: to put away opposing evidence.

we could have been happy sooner
—*Brenda Hillman*

this just in from biology:
breasts signal fitness (lateral symmetry) to potential mates

this just in from sociobiology:
the ape mother insures social standing for her daughters

      <in the language the real way I feel
        but not *separable* or *explain*, and if I
        felt otherwise, outside articulate,
        I would not, like a bad wife,
        go tearing around in constant *where is the o o o of my belief?*

                                    ⌈we are fabric, of cloth, a plucked-at knot⌉

      (are you trying to read her poems and find out if she was sleeping
        with someone or to reason the clitoris placement, whether just dreams
        or where she'd been going—)

      even science believes in modesty>

this just in:

we are happier than the poems describe

I more I, you completely ____

but we came from a code like this with themes, similar names

in the beginning the poem can be anything
but later not so many, likewise the idea:

human marriage: where human means fallible

<and despite knowing long ago that gender doesn't explain
  the exploited and less-fun mother, the wrestling father,
  physically removed husband or why———

it so appealed to us a system a code something to count on new god much more organic and when we
saw it in models we said ah yes and I always knew it and started up with metaphor and talked about
language and rhyme and adherence and valence and when they made a sheep with one mother it was
proof and when the poem seemed to have some internal logic or visceral impact and when the dogs'
eyes were so human and the other culture so like us and when a man savagely murdered his wife
we looked for him all over her severed body because we so needed every part of our bodies to be us
because it was unfashionable to say spirit this obviously valuable organism as something outside the
body god must be the ultimate protein and everywhere was suddenly proof like a seventh grade girl
knows, knows *He must notice*—>

only after, when we are in it/ incontrovertible whatever it is (this) [marriage]/ do we think to question/
how did we, did we come to be here? what, other than the simple, well-used markers, made us
made us want to?

this:
protein alone doesn't make a body or alone a body make

Darwin looked at the green disc of water surrounded by blue and knew.

The corals and coconut trees just above sea-level.
Some made sense and other pieces, he made them.

Zoophytes, polyps, and actinozoa alive in their stony shelters.

Once, trying to keep three beetles, he put one under his tongue.
When it released some vile liquid, he almost lost all.

Write it, decipher. Write it: desire.

The others believed in floods, want of floods, and famine.
The vegetable kingdom as God's green shadow.

Were we born believing?
Or, like the good giraffe, grow to seek some higher?

Adults of the same species, we use and disuse,
talk and tool-make, carve a valley.

We blast, burn, marry, reason, and with signs and gestures,
dance and drawing, make the earth subdue.

If we are animals we are not orphans.
But have not God.

If we are animals, need companions, love offspring.
Also tobacco, coffee, liquor.

If we're of animals then have not words for, nor coiled regret,
nor cunning morals.

Velum and air and in the water various cross-current similes for smother.

The actual time a heart packed in ice survives.

What the skeleton wife comes home to make for dinner.

Her fierce metabolism, narrowed profile: body, body-away.

What two men witnessed under the four-polled canopy is,
on greater magnification, how the old hag in the new mother,
fourth protein on the strand, sustains the huge placenta.

Hubris of scalpels: they never made a sheep
so lonesome as a wife.

·⟨≀⟩·

The world is full of feeble creatures in changed circumstances.

As the duck flies less, his wings diminish.

The human baby with its too big head, a homunculus addiction.

How amazing, wrote Darwin, *that the gelatinous bodies of polyps can conquer ocean waves.*

He was crazy for orchids, corals, doomed species.

I go on loving you like water but

        [That a moment can stretch and fracture, etched with fault-lines,
        tactile, tensile, but taut, like the skated-over surface of ice—]

        [When the sound of the life with small children, insatiable
        salt cravings, or wanting to be fucked to sleep—]

say: *mitochondria, the powerhouse of the cell.*

Rename misery and we have knowledge.

Young marriage-lust for zygotes makes bassinets
out of organelle cross-sections.

Mitochondria, the powerhouse of the cell.

IV. TRANSLATION

Twist sense and anti-sense strands together; cut one;
                we unwind.

It takes energy to nick the supercoiled structure hard enough—
                    (they *want* to bind)

                 but it can be broken.

We are wound, not knotted.

That we could look at this and decide the past.

That we could, that day under the chuppah, know.

That a single butterfly under the bough-lined structure, the rabbi with a glass and napkin, the
    muffled pre-sound in the crowd's minds, the groom's trembling, the bride's gold frenum.

That hydrogen binds with a polar molecule.

That the vow could move two ways in time and the characters in the drama and the audience's
    complicity and the camera's perspective and the two men watching and the scene folding up inside the album and
    the two boys on the bed wondering where they were before they were born and the mind of their mother and the
    smooth-bottomed shoe of their father and if the glass so wrapped and swaddled broke or shattered or muffled was
    the inorganic portent: sand, water, air, the compressed doctrine: an object's permanence and the social fabric the
    mind's usefulness the body's faithlessness the two-chambered heart the pornographic memory jealousy profit
    altruism patents partnerships postulates corporate metaphysics and history progress synonyms paradigms human
    mind the child's welfare.

That regret is not biological or an obstacle.

·⟐·

Photography can't account for the edge of vision, how I,
naked, make fear brilliant. The eye is not

a camera
telescope
looking glass

but all collude.

Organs don't arise from needs. Nor does cardiomegaly mean
wanderlust.

An ancient prototype of which we know nothing
passed us organs of extreme perfection
and organs of little apparent importance.

Unstoppable eye in the cranial orbit.
The giraffe's small fly-flapper.

Problems with the Central Dogma:

It doesn't allow for the promiscuity of proteins: how they seek
others.

That DNA made protein and protein made us is an attractive notion,
lovely—theorem, sermon, anodyne—and resists evidence:

chaotic cytoplasm,
clandestine mechanisms.

We understand nothing
fully, have eaten only
the ripe periphery, without
a palate for buds or boughlettes.

⚜

Feral, *more at* Fierce

The first wife was a hard-working molecule.
A ribosome without membranes making
and making unsheathed to every loving master.
By the millions she colonized the endoplasmic
reticulum, the enfolding and crenellated mitochondria.

Inside the cell: the flap and footfalls of birds and nymphs,
a dulcet hymenaeus, rushing piety.

Peppered-moths never rest on tree trunks; the textbook
photos are of dead specimens glued to sooty,
white lichen-covered bark. Nocturnal creatures,
live moths hide in the high-up canopy—

Want to know everything?

A woman's rope-like hair.
A man's clavicle, how it forms an x-axis plateau of sternum-scapula.
Our beautiful theories, their press of fealty.
The platonic tongue of wedlock.
The hush-hush palaver of optics.

Note the raised perimeter and then deduce what fell:
an edged islet I once believed bore life.

Autography

I want to change your mind. Not
you.

You're, as you are, what I want, even his
blinking neon: [no] indecision

vacancy sign. I have room
for you and these untrue

I mean disloyal
affections. I'm

a penny. Hardly
something. One

in a history of immodest
women: want, wants, wonton, I.

Autography 2

Lied. Said I'd be
satisfied with ____.

Truth is:
I want to ruin your life.

Throw them over, some
overture, ignominious

ruin, some proven—

the rest is marriage
by which we bear up

and better ourselves.

Autography 3

Shall we discuss married sex?

Yes, let's take our clothes off and talk of pros and cons, the lag and lapse. The body carries on and there's no other less-revealed. Real: the husband over or under and going forward while the mind—do you believe in it?—why speak of it?—flint-streak, it sparks and wanders, will not tame. I'm talking clearly, sincerely, when I say I saw a man and he was not my married. This he'd you. He made you he. I made you husband; it was so. We chose to.

And suppose I stayed shut-up in the always? Suppose I could have stayed shut-up like so, but o, the bad girl breeze blows in everywhere, finding the cracks and torments.

Autography 4

Today the pigeons tack
in flocks above the city.

The air is crisp, forgetful.

A plume became a cloud
became a plume became a fog,

No! I said to the TV and tried
to hold the whole thing up

before I could say stop
it—did not.

Autography 5

During this time people protested. I didn't, though I never for one moment was for it. And people bought supplies and became political but I didn't though I never for one moment doubted these necessities. A poet acquaintance had a baby. I saw her and the baby—they'd just been at a protest—and felt like I'd never had a baby despite my two boys. I stopped reading newspapers except about science and stopped the TV news though poets were at protests and writing blogs and someone asked me how I could write such abstract lyrics at a time like this and I looked at him and wondered what it felt like to write a poem. Pregnant women looked freakish to me, like costumes or experiments. On my way to the day care I looked at the big bellied women or new mothers with strollers and wondered what was it like to push a baby out of your body. Last night as I gathered my little son out of the bath into a green towel—clean, smooth, slippery, sleepy—I wondered what that was like.

A poet friend said I was writing about the shifting you in marriage. I tried to set him straight by being clearer next time. Later he said my poetry "uses slippage in point of view (between addressing a 'you' and narrating a 'he') to emphasize ambivalence about marriage, as though the speaker were struggling to keep her distance from the 'problem' and avoid using an intimate tone." So I saw then how little clear I'd been. All these problems with syntax. I'd tried to strip it, but the smooth under-bark, without its bumpy elephant skin, confused them into thinking I'd found something clean and solid. And they said I'd been hiding in science and in jargon and in metaphor and they said they liked my searing honesty but what did my husband think and they said we like this found language we like this information we like the idea of a young woman writing about her marriage but what did my husband think and when I'd written "let's discuss married sex" then I didn't, and they wanted more married sex, for the husband and wife to actually *have* sex and then someone said, but they are, right? they do, right? it's just pretty subtle and they said we want more *blatant* sex and someone said does anyone else see another *man* in these poems? And then they said science is off-putting.

Autography 7

That, between episodes, the husband,
facing the TV says *hey* . . . in a sweet way,

should not be so surprising.

"Clean me!" cries my son in his spilled water.
"Dry you," I say with my exposed shirt hem.

"Clean!" he begs, but there is no substance
to clean water.

The budding trees misstate the season.
I am astonished by my screaming offspring.

Autography 8

What the mother will not
[myriad] say. Many

to secret. This is not just

about being a woman. No one
believes mothers are, anyway.

They want to know how many
her love is

and want more.

Silence keeps them
safe so she

gives it
away: mute.

Mute, mute, mutter (her
mouth's a busted clasp).

Autography 9

My father with hardly hair on arms or legs and husband in his plush hide. I'm some other creature they look at say, *who knows what you're about?* I had a body once, remember?

My boys are two porcelain bell-sounds inside expensive, ornate eggs. Their skin is almost transparent and still soft as a breast. O ache, how the boy already starts his crossing over. Only four years old when a little boat pushed off from shore. I thought he was on it but saw then it was me, the baby-mother, floating away. We lit the craft on fire by shooting torched arrows at that mother, and told the husband in his pelts don't stand too close. Watch her burn and flicker off the edge of boyland where I've long since interloped and dug my heels in. But see here, these were only the idea of feet and I fast become an indistinct sound with indeterminate source. Murmur. Rumor.

Only a hot, palm-shaped stigma where my littler boy touches my thigh keeps me alive, staves off the specter-mother's residence.

Autography 10

In the sandbox my son pretends
to be dead. On the wooden edge I try

to look alive. I am
a wife, in other words

"woman acting
in a specified capacity" as in

"fishwife" or "mother."

What I would rather
is irrelevant other than

afterhours otherwising.

No one begged me to become
this fiery virago, ceaselessly

scraping and gutting, searching
out places to bury the wasted

entrails. One night I dug
too close and struck a root,

looked up and saw him:
—plaque nailed

to his trunk read "this one?"
—there. I must look for

something else to look for
or look at, like my boy

on his back in a box. Eyes
closed, palms up and open.

Autography 11

The woman opening to speak, to say, what can this [this]

if this is [real] then what other way of saying other are there?

It is like this. *This, everyday.*

Opened her and cracked her chest and clamped it.

Quick, we must pack it with ice, *I*

> *went to a wedding where two people loved one another*
> *they rang bells and I cried because the dancing*
> *in time everything dies except furniture my son said*
> *my intention was a little two step thinking the remedy was something similar*
> *like treating fever with marigolds or love with love but can die like that*

The spine tries to protect.

But the real this that she knows the this that the then this.

Every day. Every day. Every day.

Autography 12

What is likewise hard can cleave.

And so my roving eye sought a sharp punishment wanting the underlying shape to realize and when a man returned my wanting I made this punishment and when I wanted more punishment I looked straight at him like a blade like a punishing cleaver needing sharpening the shrill tones of the knifeman's traveling business pierce every writing through with wanting business he seeks to punish the blade I sought to punish meant to cut away the excess thereby polishing but punished the dust of the knife the cleaver the glance the gaze

Autography 13

Here, take this.

If you die it is not a good remedy. If you are healthy and develop symptoms it is a good remedy for someone else who had a sickness with these symptoms. This is the law of similars. It applies.

Writing is a way to cultivate illness. In other words torture. In other words pervade. If you die you might have had a sickness or rendezvous.

Autography 14

At night I become exquisitely pretty.

I don't want to. Seriously, I don't. Won't be convinced. Not. This time. I really, this time, I seriously. Not. Tonight. Then when you fall asleep I suddenly, well, want to. Is that what makes me beautiful?

Better pull the shades down against this blinking want-to, wasted body, the short-long-short signal I'm sending out across the city.

Autography 15

The smoke is from the falling down
I told my son who is afraid

of fire. Forgive me
for lying. One day he will find out:

the building's mangled corset,
cracked femurs and blown out lungs—

there was no one, not one,
to give our blood to. And birds

clogged the gutters. And rats. And paper.

The paper.

My son dreams of fire. He dreams
of a mouse with claws.

Meanwhile a father I know buys potassium
chloride, cipro, soup, duct tape.

Dreams of ghosts under the kitchen table.
Of his brother. Of falling.

Another man says he'd have stepped over
anyone to find his wife.

Autography 16

Things I've been asked not to write about include: the death of a young child, money, group therapy. What's the harm in an affair that never happened asks N? Therapist: when something's gone this far in the mind it means something's wrong in the marriage. We pay her and I tell them about my husband's cousin's daughter who, at two years, eight months and a matter of days

Autography 17

My son almost made but missed the toilet: that was real.

And when the night and its many beasts breathing brought him up again I said, *get back*
with your sharp bite, gorgeous fangs.

Stop writing.

It makes me visible, I meant to write invisible. Damn that night with her pester
whispering *lean* . . .
                                                    against him.

Cotton dress shirt.

I see what the stupid phrase means: "mind like a steel trap," as I gnaw my leg off to escape mine.

A reader, anonymous, suggested my poems would be better
if the marriage/motherhood stuff wasn't so literal.

Life too, I'd say.

Autography 18

I've fallen in love with everyone
to unlove him by comparison.

All men. All women.

The cross-eyed gym guy on the subway.
The woman with blond braids under her pink hat.

I have banished and exalted humor. Was
young. Old. Showed my sadness

as a corpse shows the surgeon:
see my facts of living?

For my next act I must jump off a ferry for more
good material. Right?

Somewhere, this snowy night, Spalding Gray's body
floats the Hudson, I'm certain.

Gathering material.

It's impossible to unlove some ideas.
No matter how stupid.

There he is again:
the unloved only.

Autography 19

I wanted to write a tiny poem,
but as soon as I built it, it lied.

Was the closed-mouth kiss
of marriage and children. I wanted

to leave something radiant on the pillow,
but was needed elsewhere

to proffer idioms; be stern and soothing, subtly
clairvoyant, familiar, original, over and over,

a pot boiling over puts out its fire but is still
not safe. Bough so laden

it wastes bounty. The lyric
was meant to contain desire;

I want some precious toxin.

Autography 20

One night a woman showed up.
We talked about poetry. She

was full-grown and had lived a life.

Her poems were dreams and animals,
flying objects and little wails or wafts of witchery.

She brought black bean soup from the place
downstairs and ate it at my table.

A man showed up, a younger man, another woman, but
I knew them: where they lived, if they had children.

Even her name didn't make sense and her rusted voice
made us all be quiet. She drank tea, water, seemed to be

American, but her poems moved like the clean-plucked
wing of a chicken when you run it under water: too

human. Who invited her? Later I dreamed she was riding
the express subway uptown, studying flash cards.

Don't wake up until you see the flip sides
said the dream but that

woke me up.

Acknowledgments, Dedications, and Notes

Many thanks to the editors of the following journals for publishing poems from this book: *Barrow Street, Black Warrior Review, Black Clock, Bridge, Chicago Review, Court Green, Crowd, Five Fingers Review, Gulf Coast, Lyric, Maggid, New Orleans Review, Now Culture, Tango, Xantippe,* and *Zeek.*

Seven sections from "Annunciation" were published in *Barrow Street* and won the Barrow Street prize. The poem, as a whole, was later awarded The Center for Book Arts Prize by Lynn Emanuel and was printed in a limited edition chapbook designed by Roni Grosz.

I am deeply grateful to Catherine Barnett, Arielle Greenberg, Joy Katz, Wayne Koestenbaum, D. A. Powell and Suzanna Tamminen for their generous and insightful readings of these poems.

Love and boundless appreciation for my "sisters": Joan, Arielle, Stacy, Erin, Miriam, and Dana.

•

"Squirrel in a Palm Tree" takes place en route to and from and in Savannah, Georgia, at the end of December 2001. The poem was made possible by the teachers—Eric, Rajihah, Joy, Aury, Jennifer, Rafiyah, Amanda, Martina—and Peggy at Basic Trust Day Care Center and by Lynn Heitler and Philip Levy. Thank you.

"Annunciation" is for Abram, child of light, and for Josh, Moses, and Stacy, who made the journey with me.

"Autography 6" is for Jeff Enke.

"Autography 20" is for Hermine Meinhard, John O'Connor, and Patricia Carlin.

Some of the poems are for Alex Wright.

•

". . . synonyms do not exist" is from Donald Hall's essay "The Unsayable Said," published by Copper Canyon Press.

The title, "The Museum of Accidents" refers to a proposal by French philosopher Paul Virilio for a new museum that would expose and exhibit "the accident," an inevitable consequence of our accelerated, highly technological society.

"Is the Soul just a notion, a drug?" is from Alice Notley's poem "Sun is Very Near Hot and Buttockslike" in *Disobedience*, Penguin, 2001.

"We could have been happy sooner" is from Brenda Hillman's poem "Cascadia" in *Cascadia*, Wesleyan University Press, 2001.

On page 80, "I go on loving you like water but" is from John Ashbery's poem "The Tennis Court Oath."

Other sources for "The Rise and Fall of the Central Dogma":
American Museum of Natural History, "Darwin" show, November 2005–August 2006.
Barry Commoner, "Unraveling the DNA Myth," *Harper's*, February 2002.
Benjamin Farrington, *What Darwin Really Said*, Shocken, 1966.
Sarah Blaffer Hrdy, *Mother Nature: Maternal Instincts and How They Shape the Human Species*, Ballantine Books, 1999.
Jonathan Wells, Ph.D., "Second Thoughts about Peppered Moths," http://www.arn.org/docs/wells/jw_pepmoth.htm

About the author

Rachel Zucker is the author of two previous books of poetry, *Eating in the Underworld* and *The Last Clear Narrative*, both published by Wesleyan University Press. Zucker is the co-editor of the anthology *Efforts and Affections: Women Poets on Mentorship*, published by the University of Iowa Press. She has taught at NYU and Yale and was the poet in residence at Fordham University. She lives in New York City.

www.rachelzucker.net